BILL WOODROW

Front Cover:
Armchair, Washing Machine and Kurumba Mask   1982
armchair, washing machine, metal stand and enamel paint
240×400×200 cm.
Private Collection, Paris
(BW 60)

N 0012586 5

BILL WOODROW

Sculpture 1980-86

The Fruitmarket Gallery, Edinburgh
13 September-25 October 1986

Published by The Fruitmarket Gallery

Printed in the Netherlands by Lecturis bv.

Photographs courtesy art & project, Amsterdam, Michael Arthur,
La Jolla, California, Giorgio Colombo, Milan, courtesy Eric Fabre,
Paris, Eeva-Inkeri, New York, courtesy Barbara Gladstone, New York,
courtesy Lisson Gallery, London, Jochen Littkemann, Berlin, courtesy
Heiner Bastian, Berlin, Peter McCallum, Toronto, courtesy Galerie
Nordenhake, Stockholm, Alex Saunderson, London, Bernhard Schaub,
Cologne, Edward Woodman, London, and Bill Woodrow

© 1986 The Fruitmarket Gallery and the author

ISBN 0 947912 65 7

The Fruitmarket Gallery gratefully acknowledges financial
assistance towards the exhibition from the Henry Moore Foundation

The Fruitmarket Gallery is subsidised by
the Scottish Arts Council

◀ *Self Portrait with Grey Hat*   1985
air duct, sifter, spray enamel and acrylic paint
179×72×49 cm.
Museo Tamayo, Mexico City
(BW 183)

Foreword

Bill Woodrow's sculpture has become, over the last five years, one of the most recognisable contributions to the contemporary art world. Since he first showed his new work in a temporary gallery space adjoining his studio in Brixton to an audience of his fellow-artists and critics, his constructions have been widely seen in Europe, North and South America and Australia. He has been invited to participate in international events such as the Biennales of Paris, Sao Paulo and Sydney, and the revitalised Carnegie International in Pittsburgh, and he has held one-man museum exhibitions in Oxford, Toulon, Basel and in California. But the range, vitality, wit and consistency of his work have not until now been properly documented and brought together in one publication. It is intended that this book, which accompanies a major exhibition (his second in Edinburgh) of work from the last three years, should fill this gap.

I am grateful to Lynne Cooke for her text on Bill Woodrow's work which gives it a proper context, to Nicholas Logsdail and Karsten Schubert of the Lisson Gallery, who have enabled us to present the development of Woodrow's work in this way, and most of all to Bill and Pauline Woodrow, whose photographs and records have made possible such a comprehensive documentation, and who have continually been willing to answer queries of every sort during our preparations.

The complexity, humour and gravitas of Bill Woodrow's work can be clearly seen through the chronological display of the works themselves and the explication offered by the text. Like Wyndham Lewis or Edward Burra in this century, he stands in a great line of British art which can blend the grotesque, the vernacular and popular, with subtlety and sleight of hand.

Mark Francis
Edinburgh

The Elevation of the Host

Untitled 1970
Soho Square, London

'I use images of nature as a symbol of a system which is self-regulating; if it is not interfered with it just gets on with it, and has built-in ways of controlling itself. Western industrial society appears to get the balance completely out of proportion.'[1]

Bill Woodrow's recognition of the conflict between modern society's aspirations and their impact on the world at large underpins much of the sculpture that he has made over the past six years. An assertion of his personal politics, this statement also reflects widely held views. Characteristically, it is couched in straightforward, unassuming terms, devoid of technical jargon and recondite theorising. Its laconic tone is far removed from the strident dogmatism that marked so much of the engaged art of the 70s, for to Woodrow simple answers and black and white positions are seldom possible, or desirable.

The statements made in his sculpture consequently range from the emphatic to the enigmatic: compare *Blue bird, black bomb* (page 51) which dramatically opposes its two protagonists with the mysterious symbiosis of *Pram with Fish* (page 43). On the whole, however, the content tends to be more ambivalent and more complex, as found in *Parrot Fashion* (page 91) in which a fabricated bird and pistol have been assembled from parts of a speedboat and an automobile. The recognition that all four are objects which may, on occasion, be prized as well as feared, like any attempt to discern a connecting commonality or affinity, inevitably fails to 'explain' their conjunction.

Woodrow's qualified acceptance of the post-industrial world is part of what has been deemed a

widespread anti-modernist sentiment that everywhere appears to have gripped the contemporary imagination. The sentiment is hardly limited to art, but manifests itself at every level of intellectual, cultural and political life at present. Anti-modernism is primarily a disaffection with the terms and conditions of *social* modernity, specifically, with the modernist belief in science and technology as the key to the liberation of humankind from necessity.[2]

His equivocal endorsement is expressed through a gamut of responses ranging from the wry to the ironic, the sardonic to the acerbic. There is nothing pat or simplistic in this shifting stance; on the contrary its very flexibility permits a series of skirmishes with a panoply of issues, from ecology to surveillance, militarism to rampant consumerism. Any hint of the ponderous and portentous is undermined by an intelligence that delights in the foibles and absurdities of daily life. He eschews the rhetorical and grandiloquent in favour of a disarming directness in form and mode of address, and a demotic vocabulary. If humour and fantasy were initially employed to stave off or temper an incipient pessimism, they were soon transformed into a mordant, corrosive wit that parried vigorously with its subject. Though it is generated by a sense of moral purpose, this is not a moralistic art.

Woodrow's work stems from personal experience. His imagery derives from what he encounters in daily life; whether via direct experience or through the media makes no difference. His materials are gleaned from his local environment, from what is 'to hand'; and his methods of working are, technically speaking, remarkably simple for they require neither assistants nor highly specialised equipment. (His principal implements are metal shears, pliers, hammers and an electric drill: all hand- not bench-tools.) Yet his art cannot be deemed autobiographical; he thinks in broader terms, in generalities. His imagery not only eliminates the human figure, it shuns any hint of surrogate anthropomorphism or personification in its treatment of organic and manufactured objects alike.[3] *Homo sapiens* is defined therefore not in methods derived from biology or psychology but from anthropology: that is, in terms of the relationships formed with his ambience, the material culture and the natural world at large. This approximates to an ethnologist's view-point to the extent that the material artefacts from a particular culture may serve as the evidence for the reconstruction of those underlying relationships which determine and define that society. But it was archeology, which performs a similar task for civilisations of the past, that provided the model for Woodrow's first mature statement, a series of works made in 1979. In such pieces as *Standing Stones* various domestic items—in this case a vacuum cleaner and an upright carpet sweeper—were embedded in concrete shaped to resemble rocks, and then partially excavated by cutting back, to reveal glimpses of these latter day fossils. (In several of these he introduced marble chips into the concrete to reinforce the geological character.) Punning references to the contemporary cult for megalithic sites and prehistoric remains may also be discerned. Other works which rapidly followed seem both to mirror and mock the widespread reverence, at that moment, for the so-called natural order and the remote past, in the careful laying out of the components of objects or relics, whose history was little more than instantaneous. In *Taperecorder,* for example, the combination of a geological slice and a forensic dissection has resulted in a carefully graded display

1

Untitled 1979
pinball machine, television, radio, record player, vacuum cleaner
(destroyed)

Untitled 1971
split pine trees

Standing Stones 1979
carpet sweeper, vacuum cleaner and concrete

of the machine's constituents. In others, such as *Hoover Breakdown* the dismantled original has been laid out diagnostically on the ground beside a facsimile. As Lewis Biggs has eloquently written:

> Not only does the shadow appear more real than the object from which it derives, but the machine has become its own victim—dirt waiting to be swept up. In this beautiful conceit, Woodrow . . . persuades us to believe in an object both as a result of its contiguity to the other objects, and to the degree to which we desire its function. The wooden maquette derives its reality from the dust of the floor twice over.[4]

Hoover Breakdown and several companions followed sculptures which had simply demonstrated a state of destruction and loss, as found in *4 Cleaners* in which the fragments of several objects were collected and piled into sperm or tadpole-like configurations which metaphorically suggested a new genesis without attempting to nominate its identity. From recuperation to regeneration was not a large step: it assumed various guises during the winter of 1979/80. In *Five Objects* for example, graftings from four appliances were fused to create a new one, a completely fictional entity, which at first sight proved difficult to differentiate from its peers. In *New Object,* several small appliances were embedded into the body of a freezer to produce a novel, more elaborate being. And then, in a highly prophetic sculpture *Vacuum cleaner with camera and case,* the nozzle of a vacuum cleaner was transformed into a camera. With this work Woodrow for the first time constructed a new object from the carcass of an obsolete one: previously the new entities had all been hybrids, or mongrels, of indeterminate character and function. Once again parallels might be drawn with archeology, with those attempts to reconstruct extinct objects from the fragments and shards uncovered during a dig. At times the results resemble cuckoos more than the natural progeny of the nest.

This pivotal work with the vacuum cleaner and constructed camera did not constitute a break with the sculpture of the previous months but grew directly out of methods of approach and attitudes to materials which had informed his recent work, and that of many artists in the later 70's. They had originated in a desire to close the gap between art and life by working directly with the immediate environment. Environment turned out, however, to be a notion open to enormously divergent interpretations, implying everything from the artist's body or persona, in the case of the performances of Bruce McLean and the Living Sculptors, Gilbert and George, to the physical context

which the artist inhabited. That this context should prove to be rural and the resulting work imbued with overtones of landscape and with an ideology based in notions of nature and essential truths, was not happenstance, although many of its proponents from Richard Long to Hamish Fulton, Roger Ackling and David Nash did indeed live in the English countryside. As a student at St. Martin's School of Art in the late 60's Woodrow was heir to this philosophy and aesthetic, and certain of his student works demonstrate his interest in it. For example, he devised several performances; he made films with nature as the principal motif and representation as the subject, and he created an installation from split pines arranged to form a vast organic drawing. He also executed several pieces composed of piles of elegant rocks neatly laid on the gallery floor. These painted polystyrene counterfeits parodied rather than paid homage to that pantheistic zen-like celebration of nature and the essentialising processes of time that their prototypes lauded. In another work Woodrow made a circle directly on the ground, outdoors, which ostensibly conformed to the prevailing notion of a minimal interference with the natural terrain, expressed as a fugitive intervention. The fact that it was made from pigeons devouring the grain which the artist had arranged into the appropriate shape effectively subverted this credo. Woodrow also devised a number of conceptual pieces, several of which were exhibited in international exhibitions abroad, before he virtually abandoned making objects in 1972. The diversity of the works covering those four years betrays his acute awareness of, and conditional engagement with, the prevailing debates of the day: the humorous critique symptomatic of a fundamental scepticism, and a provisional allegiance. Yet certain themes which were first employed during those years have proved to be abiding concerns: notably, questions of representation and of simulation, and the relativity of truth. When in 1978 Woodrow refurbished and equipped a studio and recommenced working his attitude to materials and to handling them proved to have altered little. It was his circumstances which had changed—and tellingly so. For he no longer spent part of the week, as he had whilst a student, living or visiting in the countryside: he was now domiciled in inner London. If, at first, the material that he gathered from the studio environs was simply 'stuff', building materials and discarded broken furniture which was readily available in quantity, cheap and relatively free from art-historical associations, it soon became evident that whilst he could insist on its neutral character, or attempt to strip it of its former identity, as occurred with the bicycle frames which he

Untitled 1971
painted polystyrene

Hoover Breakdown 1979
vacuum cleaner and wood

unravelled to form a large 'drawing' (still essentially formalist in spirit) (page 21), far greater potential lay in exploring the dialogue between the former identity of the object and its newly invented one. This provided the stimulus for *Twintub with Bicycle Frame* in which he assembled the torso of the vehicle from the casing of the domestic appliance. The result was more bizarre than the artist had anticipated, a quality which he exploited in the next four related works by heightening the realism of the new object: another bicycle, a guitar, a machine gun and a chain saw (page 27). However, the fantastic soon palled in the face of his realisation that these binary relationships could impinge on a far wider array of issues. In *Twintub with Beaver* which followed, the animal gnaws at the simulated woodgrain of the machine: visual punning now clothes an ecological statement. In *Red Squirrel* (page 23) the casing of the spin-dryer has been cut, roughly in the shape of a large leaf, to reveal the creature within, an act that might not be so surprising were this cube a block of stone, the animal carved, and the artist someone like Paul Manship or Gertrude Hermes. In Woodrow's work the act of siring, however, does not destroy the original, and the resulting relationship has a degree of 'fit', of visual and conceptual rightness, that seems more than purely serendipitous. As the range of imagery exploded so did the repertoire of raw material. In some, like *Crow and Carrion* (page 35) the found object transmogrified very closely, with the beak and wings constructed from the folds and spokes of the discarded brolly. In others, such as *Pram with Fish* (page 41), where the off-spring has been further elaborated with paint, the connection—formally as well as thematically—is far more capricious, though not quite adventitious.

Woodrow's preference for simple rapid ways of handling his material was primarily determined by his need for a technique that allowed him, as he put it "to work at a speed which is the speed at which I can 'think' about the actual work"[5]; but it also served to demystify the act of making, contributing to the directness and accessibility of the work. Both in his approach to materials and to their handling Woodrow has much in common with Tony Cragg and Richard Deacon, friends from his student days. In the late 70's all three had gathered their material from their immediate locale, devising fairly simple configurations by layering, stacking and abutting it. When in 1979 Cragg began to focus on plastic shards which he sorted and colour-coded before arranging into figurative images, like *Redskin,* a major shift occurred in his work, one which rapidly permitted an art which

addressed questions that were more than exclusively aesthetic in character. Deacon's work also expanded its frame of reference, though without recourse to a representational imagery. In the early 80's he evolved a metaphorical vocabulary of great richness and subtlety which permitted him to explore a wealth of notions through impacting, condensing and interlacing allusions that grew directly out of the material, technique and forms. Only Woodrow salvaged "white goods", domestic appliances and consumer durables, for his raw material. With them he was able both to confront issues of a specifically social character and to explore the non-discursive realms of the poetic. If the exchanges between these three sculptors were mutually beneficial, their areas of shared interest cannot be separated from the larger context, a context marked by a revival of interest in reproductive and media imagery, and a return to fixed discrete art-objects, in painting and sculpture alike, after the multi-media, temporary and site-based works of the 70's. It would be false, however, to see Woodrow and his peers as simply reacting against the predominant concerns of the previous generation. Using as an example the Statue of Liberty (conceived principally as image), Carl Andre had defined the history of twentieth century sculpture, in terms of its evolution from form to structure to place.[6] By the late 70's this abbreviated history could have been extended to encompass a fourth stage, the nexus of discourses and social relations which surrounded the monument, and which, it was argued, largely determined its meaning: 'cultural space'.[7] Where previously one definition had replaced another, in the 80's by contrast sculpture could be considered all of these at once.

Binary relationships had dominated Woodrow's work in 1981, but whether paired either in counterpoint as in *Pram with Fish* or in complicity, as found in *Bean Can with Penknife* (page 27) the binding connections generally involved synecdoche, metonomy and analogy. Although it does cut, this knife is the wrong object for opening the can, whilst the can, admittedly opened, has been pared like a fruit rather than conventionally penetrated. In the following year Woodrow expanded and complicated his approach by coupling a greater number of objects, as in *The Globe* where the flexes from an assortment of household appliances have been woven into a sphere; or by extracting several new objects from the one host, found for example in *They see, they hear, some believe.* In addition, he made a number of 'incidents', abbreviated tableaux which suggest narratives of crime and violence. *Electric Fire, Car Seat and Incident,* among the most economical, is perhaps the best: the

Electric Fire, Car Seat and Incident 1981
Installation at New 57 Gallery, Edinburgh

A Passing Car, A Caring Word 1982
bed base, car door, enamel paint

interplay between desire and danger which lies at the heart of those fantasies fed by pulp thrillers and *film noir* is here vividly encapsulated, and direct statement avoided. These potentially discursive scenarios betray affinities with the work of a number of other artists then involved with installations, but it is the differences which are ultimately more telling. For Woodrow's incidents stand somewhere between the self-contained art object and the installation proper; somewhere between an imaginative projection and actuality. They worked best, as in *Electric Fire, Car Seat and Incident,* when they reinforced the structural and material relationships linking the found and the invented components, by postulating an intrinsic instead of merely contingent relationship between the two; and when they capitalised on the distinction between the fabricated images and the found objects as partaking of different levels and types of reality. At its richest Woodrow's works establish not only a dialogue between the objects, invented and found, but a set of connections that explores the fact that they are literally, and therefore, by implication, inherently related. In mid-1982 an unprecedented monumentality and grandeur entered his work with *Car Door; Ironing Board and Twin Tub with North American Indian Head-dress* (page 39), the first of several sculptures to incorporate domestic objects and tribal imagery (see cover). The four components have been disposed so that they seem to be 'on display' rather than forming a semi-naturalistic scenario of the kind that pertains in the incidents. The 'primitive' may be here being construed as a western conception, a fabrication of the 'other': alternatively, the work may be dwelling on the plight of indigenous peoples who in seeking the material comforts of the western world are forced to banalise or sentimentalise their own culture as exchangeable commodities, as entertainment. Other readings are also possible, for Woodrow refused to endorse any one explanation. The interpretation depends on the viewpoint of the spectator, both literally and metaphorically. That it is a question of viewpoint and not of the relaying of some universal, absolute truth is intimated by the composition with its positioning of the elements as in a display, and by the physical nature of the links that bind them, links which are actual not merely hypothesised, and so counter narration with causal connections. What Woodrow has termed his recognition of the possibility of making a 'comment', (and not, significantly, a critique) flowered rapidly at this time. *A passing car, a caring word* tilts at the propensity of the media to turn disaster and death into spectacle, the microphone indicating

for Woodrow "a means by which one person—one small person—acquires great power through the technique of amplification".[8] The deadpan title plays acerbically on associations with the mafia or underworld with its stereotypical gangland killing from a speeding vehicle, as black as the related idiom "Mown down in the streets". Assassins motivated by religious and/or political fanaticism currently employ similar tactics, as seen in Lebanon, Northern Ireland and elsewhere. Woodrow wrily remarks, paraphrasing a comment that recently caught his attention: "the speeding bullet does not differentiate between the believer and the unbeliever".[9]

Blue bird, black bomb (page 49) re-presents stereotypical images whose very currency depends on their hackneyed character. The desire for an accessible imagery was less decisive for Woodrow than his recognition that social discourse in the mass-media functions via the cliché and the simplified contrast, the readymade pattern. The platitudinous may nevertheless contain truth for all that it is banal: it is simply its familiarity which renders it hackneyed. By means of a theatrical presentation which polarises the contrast between the relentless downward trajectory of the missile and the soaring flight of the bird, all played out within the parameters of mundane domesticity symbolised by the ironing board, Woodrow infuses unforgettable urgency into a banal but crucial issue: the destructiveness of humanity and its antithesis in nature.

Destruction, oppression and violence constitute the principal themes governing Woodrow's oeuvre from mid-1982 through 1983; witness *Red Telephone* (page 51) *Boeing* (page 55) and *Quattro Freccie* (page 53). Counter-examples are largely taken from the organic world, as seen in *Swan* and *Sealion* (page 59). The formal range of his work expanded in concert with the appropriation of new sources of raw material. Of these, car parts which were readily available in large supply and at low cost, were particularly suitable as they possessed substantial areas of uninflected surface, but occasional finds like the trio of trunks used in *Sound, Vision and Christ* extended his range and tested his ingenuity. In almost every case Woodrow cut and fashioned one object from another in such a way that the original retains its identity despite the mutilation, and retains its authority alongside the newcomer (although ravaged, it has a physical presence and actuality missing in the fabricated object whose reality is only skin-deep). On most occasions rather than being supplanted it remains a foil, a partner, or a counter. Seldom does one object metamorphose into another in such a way and to such a degree

Radio Tuner with Knife 1981
radio tuner

San Diego Rose 1985
artillery shell, wood, enamel and acrylic paint

that it is totally transformed: the exceptions include *Waterbird* (page 83) and *San Diego Rose*. This latter method, the one preferred by Picasso in his use of found objects, plays upon a notion central to metamorphosis, that of before and after, of a new existence *replacing* the old—though knowledge of its former character may, as in his *Bull's Head* composed from the saddle and handlebars of a bicycle, be essential to a full understanding of the meaning. By contrast it is a dialogue *between* two objects which exist at the same moment in time which is central to Woodrow's approach, a dialogue which depends upon the fact of co-existence. This in turn distinguishes him from the surrealists and their progeny who attempted through juxtaposition to effect a new reality, one that is comparable in its convulsive haunting beauty to the imaginings of the unfettered unconscious as manifest in dream and fantasy. Unlike the surrealists Woodrow's work engages with the present and the actual. He does not point to an alternative and preferred order of existence, elsewhere.

In characterising this dialogue between the found and the made object Woodrow has employed the term "host" to designate the former, implying thereby that the constructed image is its familiar correlative, a guest. In the realm of biology a more malign relationship is indicated by this term, for it refers to a plant or animal which has a parasite or commensale habitually living in it or upon it. Other interpretations of the relationship have been posited, notable that of siring, suggested both by the act of creating one from the other, and by the unsevered umbilical cord which binds the two. Other critics, however, have emphasised the destructive nature of the technique, speaking of a flaying of the skin, or the surgical cutting and dissecting of the casing. In the light of these destructive connotations a second, discrete meaning of the word "host" becomes pertinent: that of sacrificial victim. The most current usage of this alternative meaning is to be found in the context of the Christian liturgy. During the Mass or Eucharist the host, that is the bread or wafer, by an act of faith becomes the body of Christ offered to redeem sinners. Whilst this second meaning was not originally intended by the artist, its appropriateness to certain of his works such as *Tricycle and Tank* (page 31) or *Radio Tuner with Knife,* where the innocuous produces an insidious, alien or lethal off-spring, is striking.

The conjunctions of meaning, not always compatible or easily fused, which cohere around this term reflect in microcosm the interplay that Woodrow weaves around a particular theme, by means of the repetition of an emblem which is presented in

ever new contexts or is made from new substances. Two religious emblems, the Bible and the crucifixion have appeared often in his work, counterpointed at times with images redolent of the media, such as microphones, headsets, and walkie-talkies—different but equivalent forms of mental manipulation. In *Sound, Vision and Christ,* the triad of metal trunks spawns a crucifix, a walkman and a film camera, all of which are palliatives of various kinds. As Stuart Morgan argues:

> It seems to tell us something about the very nature of image making, of the need to reduce complex beliefs and emotions into a doll that can be packed away, that has no financial value whatsoever nor is it distinguishable from other factory produced religious paraphenalia. Here Woodrow's working process has allowed the Christ figure to be summoned from the case, from our beginnings—and, it is inferred, from amongst our most basic human necessities, our *mental* portmanteau. The unexpectedness of its appearance is countered by the very *rightness* of that appearance; it hangs on the wall like a contemporary altarpiece. It doesn't transcend in the way that traditional crucifixions are meant to; on the contrary, it retains all the sadness of ecclesiastical bric-a-brac.[10]

Woodrow's scepticism is not confined just to aesthetic theories which purport to be all-encompassing; it extends to those of whatever persuasion—political, military or religious—which profer consolation in the form of escape from the present and actual.

In the early 80's his art variously dwelt upon a panoply of issues arising from and addressing contemporary urban life. The diversity stemmed in part from the ways in which, without recourse to autobiography, personal experience provided the starting point for all his work. As he began to travel widely in order to make exhibitions on site, the particularities of a certain region or ambience occasionally impinged on his work. This was registered in several ways, and on several levels. At its most immediate it led to the incorporation of material and imagery that refers directly to the locale, as found for example in *Albero e Uccello* (page 77), which was made in Northern Italy from a number of olive-oil tins. Their ubiquity suggested the conceit of a reversal to raw material in the form of a tree whose fruit are the printed images found on the labels of the cans. In the summer of 1984 in New York Woodrow was unable to scavenge all his material from the streets and so sought out scrap metal yards where, not surprisingly, the bulk of suitable material proved to be

They See, They Hear, Some Believe 1982-83
wheelbarrow and enamel paint

automobile parts. That unforgettable emblem of Manhattan, the yellow cab becomes the victim of the panther's savagery in *Tattoo* (page 67). On another level, the impact of the milieu is felt less in terms of its material culture than via its social values, its mores, morals and mien, as seen in *Trivial Pursuits* (page 125). Here Woodrow conjures La Jolla, an idyllic prosperous suburb where he worked during the summer of 1985, by means of a silver Porsche door which spawns a luxuriant plant amongst whose branches may be found a gun, a closed box, and a lock around which a hummingbird hovers. Yet when each of these works is seen in the context of all the sculptures produced during that particular sojourn there is no uniformity, and no univocal statement. *Tattoo*, for example, was exhibited with *Lower East Side Lintel* (page 71) and *Cello Chicken* (page 69) amongst other works, at the Barbara Gladstone Gallery in September 1984. Moreover the specifics of any place do not confine the work to the immediate and topical; it still engages with the wider set of recurrent concerns that informs his oeuvre as a whole. It is these common reference points which establish an underlying unity, for Woodrow thinks in terms of imagery, or in response to specific objects rather than in relation to a set of ideas to be illustrated. And the authority of the ideas that inform his work derives from their basis in actuality, in real experience not in abstracted ideologies. If certain works obliquely suggest their place of origin, others have different starting points. The artist may have an image in mind which he sets out to realise; alternatively, he may be stimulated by an object that he has encountered; or some combination of both may occur. Furthermore, during its execution the work may change substantially (indicating also how crucial it is that he fabricate it himself, and not rely on assistants, or intermediaries). By mid-84 it had become apparent, nonetheless, that a recognisable vocabulary of preferred images could be identified, along with an abiding nexus of concerns. However the three fairly distinct modes which had been established early on continued to be used: work in which the 'comment' was uppermost; work which centred on a conceit, their wit a reflection of poetic precision rather than of humour per se; and thirdly, the more cryptic, allusive poetic image. These three types are exemplified respectively in *They see, they hear, some believe, Sealion,* (page 59), *Il Prete* (page 79). Their very diversity reinforces the impossibility of identifying a programmatic stance and a systematic line of attack, and confirms Woodrow's assertion that intuitive pragmatic factors determine the content if not the meaning of his work:

'it seems that the images that I've acquired are not really by choice— it's as if they have been planted in me! I'm sorting them out. Some things have more visual effect than others; that is how my work is formed: I think in terms of visual images.'[11]

Yet the constancy in themes, modes and even to a certain degree in iconography should not be overstressed. It did not, for example, prevent either a gradual shift in the types of found objects employed, nor the introduction of new themes. By mid-decade Woodrow was using fewer domestic appliances and more objects that related to office furniture and to public contexts: filing cabinets, public seating, steel ducting, even a copying machine now appear alongside the ubiquitous car doors and bonnets. And fabric, both in the form of domestic drapes and bedding, and as clothing, has recently taken a greater role than hitherto. Images that relate to security, and its correlative, 'protection' , have become more prevalent: keys and locks, the tying and binding of objects introduce questions relating to physical security, security which often proves to be excessive, futile or misguided, as found in *The Three Locks, Nature Morte* and *Mirror*. But what is interpreted on a material, literal level can clearly also be read metaphorically: intimations of the elusiveness and precariousness of such feelings as calm and peace. Indeed the natural world increasingly revealed itself as predatory, nasty and dangerous, and, in a reversal of earlier works, it becomes the violator and assailant; as seen in *Tattoo, The Key, La Lacrima,* (page 81) and *Elephant* (page 93). Counterimages to this darkling vision were relatively few, and generally disturbingly false, as found in *Hawaiian Punch* (page 75) where the exotic scenery is as cliché-ridden as a travel brochure, and just as illusory. No clear break is evident in Woodrow's work in the past half dozen years, yet there are discernible changes in emphasis and mood; most notably the shift from the stress on the daily fare of a post-industrial society to a view which implies a longer vision, one that is less insistently contemporaneous. Whilst this is reflected in the choice of certain images, such as the vanitas motif in *One Nine Eight Four* (page 95) or the scales, the conventional emblem for justice, in *The Golden Calf* (page 97), it also operates on a deeper level and is manifest in the subtle modifications in his interpretation of certain themes, notably that of death, and in the prevailing mood. The lighter side of his wit, manifest for example in *Sealion* and *Waterbird,* together with the black or sardonic timbre informing *Lower East Side Lintel* and *Fruit of the City* has been partially replaced by a quieter, more elegiac tone; and commentary,

Sebastian Brant
Das Narrenschiff 1494
woodcut from 1st published edition

Hieronymus Bosch
Ship of Fools c 1500
Musée du Louvre, Paris (photo, RMN, Paris)

however ambiguous or ambivalently stated has become ever less discursive, more impacted, and for want of a better word, 'poetic'. Symptomatic of this gradual change is the introduction of the motif of the Ship of Fools in mid-84. For Woodrow this was simply a familiar term; he was unaware of its origins, and indifferent to its genealogy in visual art. It suggested itself to him on account of its colloquial currency, as a figure of speech, and not its literary pedigree. The specific stimulus was a song by Bob Seger, which Woodrow particularly enjoys, that ends with the lone survivor of the vessel describing its final wreck:

. . . All along the fateful coast
We moved silent like a ghost
The tireless sea of timeless host possessed us
The wind came building from the cold northwest
And soon the waves began to crest
Crashing cross the forward deck
All hands lost

I alone survived the sinking
I alone possessed the tools
On that ship of fools.[12]

The fact that Woodrow chose a concept with a considerable lineage, where previously he had tended to prefer the current patois may not have been deliberate, but it was significant. The original source of the concept is Sebastian Brant's moral allegory *Das Narren Schyff*, published in 1494, which analyses the follies of mankind in verse and an accompanying series of woodcuts. Brant's tale rapidly became immensely popular, inspiring not only poetic variants but painted equivalents, of which that by Hieronymus Bosch is perhaps the most celebrated. Woodrow has employed the motif intermittently, some half dozen times, on each occasion siting it differently, and using different raw materials. But in every case its makeshift character, and embattled condition accord well with Brant's (and Seger's) concept of a barque in poor repair driven fruitlessly and futilely by a band of incompetents.[13]

The sense of impending disaster informing many of Woodrow's earlier works gradually gives way to a less dramatic but more encompassing sense of mortality. In many of his earlier works, like *Red Telephone* or *Electric Fire, Car Seat and Incident* the feeling of lurking danger or incipient violence was signalled in the unhooked telephones, the pools of blood, the discarded bullets. When the organic world also proved to be predatory, as in *Tattoo* and *Elephant* the momentary and circumstantial were

replaced by the generic and recurrent. Most recently, in place of destruction and violence, folly now reigns. As seen in *Fools' Coats* (page 127) it is once again divorced from a specific situation and moment in time. The futility and stupidity of man's activities rather than their innate turpitude tends now to dominate Woodrow's vision, a vision which has much in common with that of Brant, who summarized his position in the following terms:

The whole world lives in darksome night,
In blinded sinfulness persisting,
While every street sees fools existing
Who know but folly, to their shame,
Yet will not own to folly's name.
Hence I have pondered how a ship
Of fools I'd suitably equip . . .
Who sees his image on the page
May learn to deem himself no sage,
Nor shrink his nothingness to see,
Since none who lives from fault is free.
Whoe'er his foolishness decries
Alone deserves to rank as wise.[14]

Increasingly in Woodrow's work mortality is perceived as unavoidable, because inevitable, rather in terms of the unique and circumstantial event. Thus a metaphysical view replaces an historical one. At the point where a broader vision subsumes a socio-cultural commentary the analogy with anthropology breaks down. A new model of the artist must be posited, one that approximates to the fabulist rather than the ethnologist.

Woodrow's work has to date generally been interpreted synchronically, that is, in relation to issues current in contemporary culture. Barthes has been invoked, along with Baudrillard, and in ways that underscore the prevalence of signs and simulacra in the sculptor's practice.[15] Objects are read as images (and images as objects) rather than simply as the sloughed off remains of a spent consumerism. Both the two- and three-dimensional forms belong to conventionalised codes of representation, manifestations of visual imagery by mass reproduction which renders all images, from whatever culture or era, available and equivalent. As Nena Dimitrijevic has argued, the contemporary artist

is well aware of his post-industrial electronic environment and its unlimited possibilities for the assimilation, deposit and retrieval of images. The fact that we live in a new age of image sanctification in which the work becomes an interplay

Pablo Picasso
Tête de Femme 1929-30
Musée Picasso, Paris (photo: RMN, Paris)

Max Beckmann
Still-Life with Musical Instruments 1930
Städtische Galerie, Frankfurt

of signs that demand to be read and deciphered, has caused a shift of focus in sculpture from object to image, from the thing itself to its appearance.[16] References to the theories of any particular philosopher are, however, unnecessary, for such arguments have become widely dispersed and assimilated. By contrast, there have been relatively few attempts to locate Woodrow's work within western artistic traditions. Accounts of his place within the history of the twentieth century art have tended to elucidate the circumstances in which his aesthetic matured, the milieu of the late 70's, and his affinities with contemporaries such as Cragg and Deacon. Parallels with peers abroad who employ a similar range of imagery or a like attitude to materials have also been suggested, notably a comparison with Morley and Kiefer (but tellingly, not Salle or Longo) on the grounds that Woodrow uses consumer imagery for an ethically orientated statement rather than for purposes of deconstruction.[17] Closer in spirit and tenor is the work of Jenny Holzer who employs homilies, truisms, platitudes and colloquialisms in tones that range from the bantering to the virulent in order to impart her messages and warnings.

More wide-sweeping attempts to locate Woodrow's work have concentrated on the role of the found object in twentieth century art, from Duchamp's nominated ready-mades to Schwitters' redeemed objects, to Picasso's metamorphoses. Yet such comparisons are misplaced, for it is not the object per se that lies at the heart of Woodrow's work, but the manner in which the relationships between objects/images reveal aspects of the values and beliefs of their makers and users. The quintessential mode for this is the still-life.

In western painting the still-life burgeoned as a distinct genre during the late Renaissance, quickly devolving into several types, including the memento mori, and the celebration of the physical world. In the nineteenth century implicit and explicit allegory gave way to a fully secularised, unencumbered focus on pictorial problems, for which the still-life amongst all the genres was the best fitted. In the twentieth century many artists have developed further its tacit freedom to arrange and order the physical world at will, to the extent of contravening even its fundamental laws. De Chirico pioneered the imaginary still-life in which objects that would normally have no logical relationship together were juxtaposed, often in front of a background that bore no discernable relationship to them. If he opened the way for surrealist fantasies, De Chirico also foreshadowed an alternative extension of the still life, one that brought objects together in an invented or abstracted space, not to conjure the marvellous, but in order to make a statement. Beckmann is perhaps the quintessential exponent of this mode, and not surprisingly allegory and vanitas imagery play a large part in his vocabulary. In such paintings as *Large Still Life with Telescope* (1927) and *Still Life with Musical Instruments* (1930) the connections between the objects although far from realistically accountable, are not registered as implausible, but as consequential. Allegory serves as the umbrella under which such juxtapositions of disparate material may be interpreted, and provides the key for decoding the imagery. Traditional vanitas motifs, like the candle, musical instruments, cut flowers, mirror, book and globe allude to the transience of earthly pleasures and the vanity of sensory delights. The degree to which Woodrow's lexicon adheres, albeit unconsciously, to traditional vanitas iconography is striking.[18] Even the methods of composing that he prefers recall those proper to still life, now realised in three dimensions.

It was not until the early twentieth century that still-life became a subject for sculpture.[19] Its subsequent history has proved intermittent and limited, notwithstanding such remarkable examples as Picasso's cubist constructions and later pieces such as *Bottle with Goat's Skull* or the numerous works by more recent artists such as Lichtenstein and Dubuffet. (It is perhaps telling that these three artists are principally painters who have on occasion turned to sculpture as an extension of their two-dimensional work.) The format of a considerable number of Woodrow's works, particularly those located against or on a wall like *Sunset* (page 101), *One Nine Eight Four* (page 95) and *Flame* and those which utilise the car bonnet as a plane, backdrop or foil, like *Red Telephone* (page 51), *Table* (page 72), *Locust and Reliquary* (page 73), and *Cactus and Calculator* clearly recall pictorial antecedents of the type epitomised in Juan Gris' *The View Across the Bay* (1921) where a table with objects is placed before an open window or Picasso's *Still Life with Skull, Leeks and Pottery* (1945) in which the ensemble of familiar objects sets up a highly charged atmosphere. Others, like *Soupe du Jour* (page 87), *The Glass Jar* (page 85), and *Charm* actualise objects which formerly would have been rendered illusionistically, as seen in Ensor's still-life *The Ray* or Chardin's *Hare and Copper Cauldron*. Less straightforward but arguably still within the purlieu of still-life are those works in which the objects are not contiguous but are nevertheless linked, as occurs in *Kimono* (page 57) and *Time and Place for Nothing* (page 117). Here the presence of the filial ties, the visible signs of their genesis, serves

8

Mirror 1984
vacuum cleaner and mirror

Flame 1984
telephone relay box and enamel paint

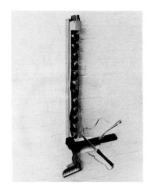

Hammer Plate 1984
telephone relay box and enamel paint

to distinguish them from installation works and assemblages which occupy real space and are to be interpreted literally, as an extension of the viewer's world, often to the point of involving the spectator physically, as with Kienholz's Beanery, for example. The selective realism which Woodrow employs, a realism that from the second washing machine with bicycle of 1980, has always been qualified, never hyper-realist, reinforces their distinctiveness and separateness as objects, or species. Sculpture is for Woodrow a distinct category, different from everyday reality. Not only does he recognise that the context in which a work of art is apprehended shapes its meaning, but he forestalls any suggestion that art might cross or dissolve the boundary into life by acknowledging the differences between the two, formally as well as conceptually. In this he differs fundamentally from many other artists who use found objects. Far from constructing a spurious pedigree for his work, recognition of its affinities with previous still-life painting, and of the recurrence of vanitas imagery, serves to illuminate certain of the ways in which he addresses issues that are perennial in western culture. It also reconfirms the claim that his work has a depth and pertinence that extends beyond the merely contemporaneous.

Mirror eloquently demonstrates the manner in which he engages with traditional concerns in contemporary guise. A vacuum cleaner sprouts a butterfly (a conventional symbol of the soul), a watch whose face is visible only in the reflection of a cracked mirror on the ground below (time's inexorable passage) and a bunch of keys held aloft by the erect hose (the futility of gestures of permanence and safe-keeping). The appliance forms a kind of free-standing pivot from which these various items are cantilevered into space: on this occasion it is of relatively little importance in itself, serving principally as a structural member and material source. All the manufactured items are commonplace, and all have been made from familiar matter, the casing of the appliance. That they were actually constructed by the artist, and not simply accumulated, is crucial, as is the format of the composition. Though these new objects are based on familiar objects in the material world, they are fabricated copies, not the real thing. Their conjunction and placement does not conform to reality, it has clearly been governed by the subjective wishes of the artist. These still-life objects inhabit an artificial abstracted space, one that in defying reality decontextualises them. The resulting autonomy facilitates the setting up of an alternative, internal ordering, a self-referencing interplay that

though it does not ape the world outside is nonetheless cogent and meaningful. Although it has its roots in the material world, this sculpture occupies a middle ground, between the subjective and the objective, the actual and the simulated, a position which divorces it from reality and situates it in the realm of the aesthetic and ahistorical. This establishing of an ahistorical, abstract mode within a realist language, this extracting of the work from the particulars of time and space, together with the substitution of an emblematic cross-referencing in place of narrative connections, is central to Woodrow's work. It allows his objects to take on a kind of 'absolute' existence of their own, separate, and decontextualised yet tied together into an autonomous whole. Their precarious equivocal form of realism verges on allegory at times, and at others, establishes contrasts and polarities, hypostatised into the antimonies of nature and culture, the rural and the urban, the savage and the civilised, without, however, undermining or disrupting this disasociated, internally refractive and subjectively ordered matrix. It begets a generalised, mythic statement, one that is powerfully expressive without fixing definitive meanings. Objects like the watch and keys recur frequently in Woodrow's oeuvre. By means of repetition, variation and permutation, he orchestrates expressive constellations that accrue in resonance and subtlety as their pedigree lengthens.

Yet not all Woodrow's work can be discussed within the format of the still-life. In addition to the 'incidents', and several quasi-installations, including *Life on Earth*, and *Ship of Fools: The Discovery of Time*, there are a group of elaborate *mise-en-scènes*, monumental works such as *The Golden Rule* (page 135), *Shrine, Stone Wall* and *Still Waters* (page 123) whose imagery, format and perhaps scale which takes them almost into the realm of the monument preclude this. Bosch's rendition of the Ship of Fools would have to be termed a *capriccio* by his contemporaries, a fantasy with an ethical content that reflected a personal vision of the world. Whether in the work of Bosch or of Goya, another of its principal exponents, the *capriccio* incorporates folkloric and proverbial material and a savage wit without jeopardising its moral character. It is thus very far from the free fantasy of surrealism, which deliberately seeks to contravert ethical and aesthetic values. In addition to those that incorporate the ship of fools many of Woodrow's larger tableaux can be seen in this light, though this does not imply that their moral content can be stated in any straightforward discursive fashion. Allegory sometimes is evident, as in *Switch* (page 131) which employs traditional emblems such as the sickle, but more often their modern counterparts have been substituted—the clock for the hourglass, the lightbulb for the candle, the abandonned jacket for the skull—and the vernacular replaces the folkloric, and the colloquial the proverbial. If juxtapositions of the kind that occur in *Promised Land* (page 129), between the piano and the tree with its crop of lugubrious coats like a genealogical emblem of death do not appear bizarre or fantastical, and are not experienced as surreal, this is because distinctions between the actual and the imagined, the literal and the suppositional are irrelevant and inappropriate. As Richard Prince put it in a recent story:

> Unbelievable and believable have become the same thing. Any viewpoint is as good as any other. They used to call it relativity, and now they call it the closest thing to the real thing.[20]

Of course this does not mean that such distinctions cannot be drawn, but simply that there are many modes with considerable currency at present which collapse such distinctions. In the realm of literature, for example, authors of the calibre and seniority of Borges and Calvino have helped pave the way for several generations of writers of very diverse types, from Marquez to Puig to the Martian Poets, all of whom demolish such barriers, albeit to very different ends.[21] In the visual arts, by contrast, that which is not logical and rational is too often simplistically dubbed surrealist. Woodrow's work demonstrates the poverty and reductiveness, the limitations, of these conventional types of categorizing. He suggests that the differences between direct and mediated, synthetic and immediate experience may at times be irrelevant, or at the least inconsequential. The interplay between these two spheres may generate poetic truths (as distinct from analytic critique), truths which open the way to imaginative speculation. Artists from the past may serve as precedents, providing paradigms by which other facets of his sculpture can be explored.

In several of Woodrow's recent works, amongst his finest to date, there is a renewal of the compact, distilled quality that characterised certain of his early, now "classic" pieces: compare *Twintub with Guitar, Crow and Carrion, Armchair, Washing machine and Kurumba Mask* with *Winter Jacket, Achtung!* and *Promised Land*. Although all are replete with a visual poetry that is distinctly his own, there has been a noticeable shift in its character toward something grander and more elegiac. Woodrow does not regard his work as pessimistic, indeed he speaks of a

qualified optimism, and delights in the recuperation of what was abandoned and spurned.[22] But a latent fatalism, which runs deeper than notions of optimism and pessimism, and which surfaces in the recurrent vanitas imagery, has resulted recently in the elusive yet haunting spirit of melancholia permeating these meditative works. Writing on the subject of transience, Freud observed that an awareness of the ephemerality of all things may serve to render them only the more valuable and desirable to the observer; alternatively, it may confirm in him or her a tendency to mourning and melancholia.[23] An authentically tragic vision has had little currency in the twentieth century: the absurd has become its modern equivalent. If *Achtung!* recalls the lyrical pathos which suffuses the writing of Borges, *Promised Land* is replete with the spirit of Beckett. Bordered on the one flank by an oneiric introspection and on the other by a mordant resilience, the vast terrain which Woodrow is mapping in his work is singular, full of areas hitherto unexplored, and of riches unforeseen.

Lynne Cooke

1. Statement to the author, July 1986.

2. Craig Owens, 'Honor, Power and the Love of Women', *Art in America,* January 1983, p. 11.

3. At the time of writing there are three exceptions to this, *Shadow of the Circus,* 1985 which contains a human silhouette, and two self-portraits, which are obliquely figural; the first by means of a hat, and the second through the device of a jack-in-the-box.

4. Lewis Biggs, 'Bill Woodrow: The Desiring Machine', in *Transformations: New Sculpture From Britain,* XVII Bienal de Sao Paulo, 1983, The British Council, pp. 62-64.

5. Quoted in *Space Invaders,* The Mackenzie Art Gallery, University of Regina, Regina, Saskatchewan, 1985, p. 90.

6. Carl Andre, quoted in *Carl Andre: Sculpture 1959-78,* Whitechapel Art Gallery, London, 1978, n.p.

7. Rosalind Krauss used this term to indicate "a public conventional realm", ref. Rosalind E. Krauss, *Passages in Modern Sculpture,* (1977), MIT Press, Cambridge, 1983, p. 266.

8. See note 1.

9. See note 1.

10. Stuart Morgan 'Loose Talk', in *The Sculpture Show,* The Arts Council of Great Britain, London, 1983, p. 97.

11. Quoted in *Space Invaders,* op. cit. p. 93.

12. Bob Seger 'Ship of Fools', from the album *Night Moves.*

13. In *Madness and Civilisation: A History of Insanity in the Age of Reason* (1961) Tavistock Publications, 1982, ch. 1, Michel Foucault discusses the image of the Ship of Fools: its relation to vanitas imagery may be gauged from the following statement: "Something new appears in the imaginary landscape of the Renaissance; soon it will occupy a privileged place there: the Ship of Fools . . . The *Narrenschiff,* of course, is a literary composition probably borrowed from the old Argonaut cycle . . . whose crew of imaginary heroes, ethical models, or social types embarked on a great symbolic voyage which would bring them, if not fortune, then at least the figure of their destiny or their truth . . . But of all these romantic or satiric vessels the *Narrenschiff* is the only one that had a real existence—for they did exist, these boats that convoyed their insane cargo from town to town . . . It is possible that these ships of fools, which haunted the imagination of the entire early Renaissance, were pilgrimage boats, highly symbolic cargoes of madmen in search of their reason . . . why so abruptly in the fifteenth century is the theme suddenly formulated in literature and iconography? . . . Because it symbolised a great disquiet, suddenly dawning on the horizon of European culture at the end of the Middle Ages.

Up to the second half of the fifteenth century, or even a little beyond, the theme of death reigns alone. The end of man, the end of time, bears the face of pestilence and war. What overhangs human existence is this conclusion and this order from which nothing escapes . . . Then in the last years of the century this enormous uneasiness turns in on itself; the mockery of madness replaces death and its solemnity. From the discovery of that necessity which inevitably reduces man to nothing, we have shifted to the scornful contemplation of that nothing which is existence itself. Fear in the absolute limit of death turns inward in a continuous irony; man disarms it in advance, making it an object of derision by giving it an everyday tamed form, by constantly renewing it in the spectacle of life, by scattering it throughout the vices, the difficulties, the absurdities of all men. Death's annihilation is no longer anything because it was already everything, because life itself was only futility, vain words, a squabble of cap and bells . . . Madness is the *déjà-là* of death. But it is also its vanquished presence, evaded in those everyday signs, which announcing that death reigns already, indicate that its prey will be a sorry prey indeed . . .

The substitution of the theme of madness for that of death does not mark a break, but rather a torsion within the same anxiety. What is in question is still the nothingness of existence, but this nothingness is no longer considered an external, final term, both threat and conclusion; it is experienced from within as the continuous and constant form of existence. And where once man's madness had been not to see that death's term was approaching, so that it was necessary to recall him to wisdom with the spectacle of death, now wisdom consisted of denouncing madness everywhere, teaching men that they were no more than dead men already, and if the end was near it was to the degree that madness, become universal, would be one and the same with death itself.
(I am grateful to Lewis Biggs for drawing my attention to this text.)

14. Sebastian Brant, *Das Narren Schyff, The Ship of Fools,* translated by Edwin H. Zeydel, New York, 1944, P. 57-8.

15. See, for example, Michael Newman, "Bill Woodrow", *Art Monthly,* No. 53, Feb. 1982.

16. Nena Dimitrijevic, 'Sculpture and its double, towards a definition of post-evolutionary sculpture', in *The Sculpture Show,* op. cit. p. 138.

17. See Mark Francis, "Bill Woodrow: Material Truths", *Artforum,* Jan. 1984, pp. 34-38.

18. There are few direct and deliberate quotations of particular art-works from the past in Woodrow's work, because, he says, it impinges little on his daily life and so plays little part in his thinking. Contemporary music, by contrast, frequently provides themes, and even at times titles, as found in *Promised Land,* taken from a Chuck Berry song of that name (though Woodrow actually prefers Johnnie Allan's rendition) and Seger's *Ship of Fools,* discussed above.

19. Picasso is a major exponent of the still-life in sculpture and of the use of the found object in art. Though the two often coincide in his work, and elsewhere, they are distinct traditions nonetheless.

20. Richard Prince 'Anyone Who is Anyone', *Parkett,* No. 6, 1983, p. 67.

21. Comparisons between Woodrow's work and the Martian Poets have been made several times, first by John Roberts in 'Urban Renewal (New British Sculpture)', *Parachute,* No. 30, March 1983. John Bayley writes of the Martian Poets "Like Craig Raine, he (Christopher Reid) has the gift of defamiliarisation which demands the familiar knowledge of the reader's eyes . . . In practice, this technique is probably as old as poetry, consisting as it does not of an idea and object abstractly yoked for exemplary purposes, as in the Metaphysical conceit, but of two objects magicked into a coincidence that produces not visual fantasy but homely truth." ("Decorations and Contingencies", *The London Review of Books,* 16 September-6 Oct. 1982, p. 14.)

22. When asked directly about this Woodrow commented: "What appears to be a preoccupation with death has not been conscious on my part. The issues that result in death are the ones that worry us most. Death is not necessarily something that I am preoccupied with, but it *is* something with which the world is preoccupied. If you watch television for an evening, the subject that comes up most is death, directly or indirectly, whether it is a western or the news reports." quoted in *Space Invaders,* op. cit. p. 93.

23. Sigmund Freud 'On Transience', reprinted in *The Pelican Freud Library,* No. 14, Penguin, Harmondsworth, 1985, pp. 283-290.

BILL WOODROW

Born 1948, England. Lives in London

1967-68
Winchester School of Art, Winchester.

1968-71
St. Martin's School of Art, London.

1971-72
Chelsea School of Art, London.

One-man Exhibitions:
1972
Whitechapel Art Gallery, London.

1979
Künstlerhaus, Hamburg.

1980
The Gallery, Acre Lane, London.

1981
LYC Gallery, Banks, Cumbria.
New 57 Gallery, Edinburgh.
Galerie Wittenbrink, Regensburg.

1982
Lisson Gallery, London.
Kunstausstellungen, Stuttgart.
Galerie Eric Fabre, Paris.
St. Paul's Gallery, Leeds.
Ray Hughes Gallery, Brisbane.
Galerie 't Venster, Rotterdam.
Michele Lachowsky Gallery, Antwerp.

1983
Franco Toselli Gallery, Milan.
Museum van Hedendaagse Kunst, Gent.
Lisson Gallery, London.
Museum of Modern Art, Oxford.
Barbara Gladstone Gallery, New York.
Locus Solus, Genova.
art + project, Amsterdam.

1984
Mercer Union, Toronto.
Musée de Toulon, France.
Paul Maenz, Cologne.

1985
Kunsthalle Basel, Switzerland.
Barbara Gladstone Gallery, New York.
Donald Young Gallery, Chicago (with Anish Kapoor).
Natural Produce, An Armed Response, La Jolla Museum of
Contemporary Art, California (touring).

1986
Galerie Nordenhake, Malmö.
Paul Maenz, Cologne.
Butler Gallery, County Kilkenny.
The Fruitmarket Gallery, Edinburgh.
Lisson Gallery, London.

Group Exhibitions:
1971
Art Systema, Museum of Modern Art, Buenos Aires.
Art as an Idea in England, CAYC, Buenos Aires.

1972
3rd Biennale of Colombia.
Platform '72, Museum of Modern Art, Oxford.

1973
Drawing, Museum of Modern Art, Oxford.

1981
An International Show of Fourteen New Artists, Lisson Gallery,
London.
Objects and Sculpture, Arnolfini, Bristol/I.C.A., London.
The Motor Show, Front Room, Percy Road, London.
Through the Summer, Lisson Gallery, London.
British Sculpture in the 20th Century, Whitechapel Art Gallery,
London.

1982
Sydney Biennale.
South Bank Show, South London Art Gallery, London.
Neue Skulptur, Gallerie Nächst St. Stephan, Vienna.
Lecons de Choses, Kunsthalle, Berne/Musee d'Art et d'Histoire,
Chambéry/Maison de la Culture, Chalon sur Saone.
Venice Biennale.
Englische Plastik Heute/British Sculpture Now, Kunstmuseum,
Lucerne.
Paris Biennale.
Prefiguration, Centre d'Art Contemporain, Chambéry.
London/New York—1982, Lisson Gallery, London.
Objects and Figures, Fruitmarket Gallery, Edinburgh.
Vol de Nuit, Galerie Eric Fabre, Paris.

1983
Tema Celeste, Museo Civico d'Arte Contemporanea, Gibellina.
La Trottola di Sirio, Centro d'Arte Contemporanea, Siracusa.
A Pierre et Marie (Phase 1), Rue d'Ulm, Paris.
Truc et Troc, ARC Musee d'Art Moderne de la Ville de Paris,
Paris.
Figures and Objects, John Hansard Gallery, Southampton.
La Grande Absente, Musee d'Ixelles, Brussels.
A Pierre et Marie (Phase 2), Rue d'Ulm, Paris.
Necessites, Chateau de la Roche Jagu, France.
Australian Perspecta 1983, Art Gallery of New South Wales,
Sydney.
Beelden 1983, Rotterdam.
Forme e Informe, Bologna.
A Pierre et Marie (Phase 3), Rue d'Ulm, Paris.
Reseau Art 83, Art Prospect, France.
The Sculpture Show, Hayward/Serpentine Gallery, London.
*L'Estate del 1983 fu Straordinariamente Lunga e Fresca: Senza
Precedenti,* Marciana.
Arcaico Contemporaneo, Museo del Sannio, Benevento.
Best of . . . , Le Coin du Miroir, Dijon.
New Art at the Tate Gallery, London.
Costellazione, Galleria Giorgio Persano, Turin.
Transformations, Sao Paulo Biennale XVIII, Brazil.
As Of Now, Walker Art Gallery, Liverpool/Douglas Hyde
Gallery, Dublin.
La Imagen del Animal, Madrid.

A Pierre et Marie (Phase 5), Rue d'Ulm, Paris.

1984
Salvaged, P.S.I., New York.
An International Survey of Recent Painting and Sculpture,
Museum of Modern Art, New York.
Skulptur im 20 Jahrhundert, Merian Park, Basel.
Contemporary Acquisitions, Imperial War Museum, London.
Nuit et Jour, Salle Gatier et Cave des Sources, Boen, France.
Terrae Motus 1, Fondazione Amelio, Ercolano, Naples.
Through the Summer 1984, Lisson Gallery, London.
Home and Abroad, Serpentine Gallery, London.
ROSC '84, The Guinness Hop Store, Dublin, Eire.
Bienale van de Kritiek, Antwerp, Belgium.
Sculptures dans L'Usine, Comite d'Establissement Renault,
Sandouville, Le Havre, France.
Musée des Beaux Arts Andre Malraux, Le Havre, France.
The British Art Show, Arts Council touring City Museum and Art
Gallery, Ikon Gallery, Birmingham/Royal Scottish Academy,
Edinburgh/Mappin Art Gallery, Sheffield/Southampton Art
Gallery.
Armed, Interim Art, London.
Deux Regions en France, L'art International d'aujourdhui, Palais
des Beaux Arts, Charleroi, Belgium.
Opere su Carta 1984, Centro d'Arte Contemporanea, Siracusa,
Italy.

1985
Space Invaders, Mackenzie Art Gallery, Regina, Canada.
Images of War, Chapter, Cardiff.
The British Show, British Council touring: Art Gallery of Western
Australia, Perth/Art Gallery of New South Wales, Sydney/
Queensland Art Gallery, Brisbane/Melbourne/New Zealand.
7000 Eichen, Kunsthalle Tübingen, W. Germany.
Sculptures du Frac Rhône-Alpes, Musée Sainte Croix, Poitiers.
Nouvelle Biennale de Paris 85
Drawing: Paintings & Sculpture, Brooke Alexander Inc., New
York
Recent Acquisitions, Modern Museet, Stockholm.
Social Studies, Barbara Gladstone Gallery, New York.
Anniottanta, Assessorato alla Cultura del Commune di Ravenna
(Bologna, Imola, Romagna).
20 Sculptures du Rhône-Alpes, l'Abbaye de Tournus (touring).
Attitudes, Central Gallery, Northampton.
Currents, I.C.A. Boston, Massachusetts.
Sculptures, Fondation Cartier, Paris.
The Irresistible Object: Still Life 1600-1985, Leeds City Art
Galleries.
1985 Carnegie International, Museum of Art, Pittsburgh.
Entre el Objeto y la Imagen, Palacio de Velazquez, Madrid/
Barcelona (British Council).

1986
9 Artists from Britain, Louisiana Museum, Humlebaek,
Denmark.
Project for the Mattress Factory, Pittsburgh, USA.
Englische Bildhauer, Galerie Harald Behm, Hamburg.
British Sculpture, Museum of Contemporary Art, Chicago and
Touring.

SELECTED BIBLIOGRAPHY

Bill Woodrow, edited interview with Iwona Blaszczyk, Objects and Sculpture (cat.), I.C.A., London and Arnolfini Gallery Bristol, 1981.

William Feaver, *An air of light relief*, The Observer, London, 28 June 1981.

Thomas Lawson, *Reviews: Edinburgh, Bill Woodrow New 57 Gallery*, Artforum vol. XX No. 4, New York, December 1981.

Waldemar Januszczak, Bill Woodrow, The Guardian, London, 14 January 1982.

Michael Newman, *Bill Woodrow*, Art Monthly No. 53, London, February 1982.

Caroline Collier, *Reviews: London, Bill Woodrow, Lisson Gallery*, Flash Art No. 106, Milan, February/March 1982.

John Roberts, *Car doors and Indians*, ZG No. 6, London, April 1982.

Bill Woodrow, edited interview with Catherine Ferbos, Leçon des Choses (cat.), Kunsthalle, Bern, 1982.

Michael Newman, *Bill Woodrow and the excavation of the object*, Englische Plastik Heute (cat.), Kunstmuseum, Luzern, 1982.

Michael Newman, *New Sculpture in Britain*, Art in America, No. 7, New York, September 1982.

Demetrio Paparoni, La Trottola di Sirio (cat.), Centro d'Arte Contemporanea, Siracusa and the British Council, 1983.

John Roberts, *Urban renewal, new British sculpture*, Parachute No. 30, Montreal, March 1983.

William Feaver, *Salvage into sculpture*, The Observer, London, 24 April 1983.

David Elliott, *The sculpture of Bill Woodrow*, Beaver, Bomb and Fossil (cat.), Museum of Modern Art, Oxford, 1983.

Waldemar Januszczak, *A nasty shock for the still-life*, The Guardian, London, 10 June 1983.

Marco Livingstone, *Reviews: Bill Woodrow at the Lisson Gallery*, Art-scribe No. 41, London, June 1983.

Alain Cueff, *Bill Woodrow*, Artistes No. 16, Paris, June 1983.

Enrico Comi, Arcaico Contemporaneo (cat.), Museo del Sannio, Benevento and the British Council, 1983.

Lewis Biggs, *The desiring machine*, Transformations (cat.), the British Council for the Bienal de Sao Paolo, 1983.

Mark Francis, *Bill Woodrow: Material truths*, Artforum, New York, January 1984.

Jerry McGrath, *Reviews: Bill Woodrow, Roland Brener*, Vanguard, Canada, May 1984.

Trevor Gould: *Reviews: Roland Brener, Bill Woodrow*, Parachute, Montreal, June 1984.

Michael Newman, interview with Bill Woodrow, Terrae Motus (cat.), Napoli, June 1984.

Rita Pokorny, *Bill Woodrow, a talk*, Neue Kunst in Europa No. 4/1, München, June 1984.

Jon Thompson, *Critical attitudes*, The British Art Show (cat.), Orbis publishing and the Arts Council of Great Britain, November 1984.

Jean-Christophe Ammann, Bill Woodrow (cat.), Kunsthalle, Basel, January 1985.

Sandy Nairne and Bruce Ferguson, Space Invaders (cat.), MacKenzie Art Gallery, University of Regina, Canada, February 1985.

Goschka Gawlik, *Bill Woodrow: Mülltheorie aus Blech*, Falter, Wien, February 1985.

William Feaver, The British Show (cat.), Art Gallery of New South Wales, Sydney, February 1985.

David Britton, *A show has its shocks*, The West Australian, Perth, 15 February 1985.

Ted Snell, *Relevance strikes a blow for the British*, The Australian, Sydney, 21 February 1985.

One city a patron (cat.), Scottish Arts Council, February 1985.

Heiner Bastian, *Bill Woodrow*, 7000 Eichen (cat.), 1985.

Joan Borsa, *Space invades*, Vanguard, Canada, May 1985.

Nouvelle Biennale de Paris (cat.), 1985

David Joselit, *Bill Woodrow*, Currents No. 6, The Institute of Contemporary Art, Boston, September 1985.

Lynda Forsha, Natural Produce, an Armed Response (cat.), La Jolla Museum of Contemporary Art, California, October 1985.

Sculptures (cat.), Fondation Cartier, October 1985.

The Irresistible Object (cat.), Leeds City Art Galleries, October 1985.

Lewis Biggs, Entre el Objeto y la Imagen (cat.), Ministerio de Cultura, Spain and the British Council, January 1986.

Lynne Cooke, *Bill Woodrow*, Artics 2, Barcelona, January 1986.

Ciaran Carty, *Junk as art*, Colour Tribune, Dublin, 2 February 1986.

Waldemar Januszczak, *Britain seen from the south*, The Guardian, London, 26 February 1986.

Kenneth Baker, *Review: La Jolla/Berkeley*, Artforum, March 1986.

Oystein Hjort, *Britain seen from the north*, Louisiana Revy, 1986.

Lynne Cooke, *Review*, Figura, Madrid.

Five Objects   1979/80
radio, record players, electric kettle and toy clothes iron
25×140×50 cm.
Private Collection
(BW 10)

New Object   1979/80
television, freezer, oven, food mixer, record player and electric drill
Destroyed

Eight Bicycle Frames   1980
bicycle frames
600×1200×40 cm.
Private Collection
(BW 23)

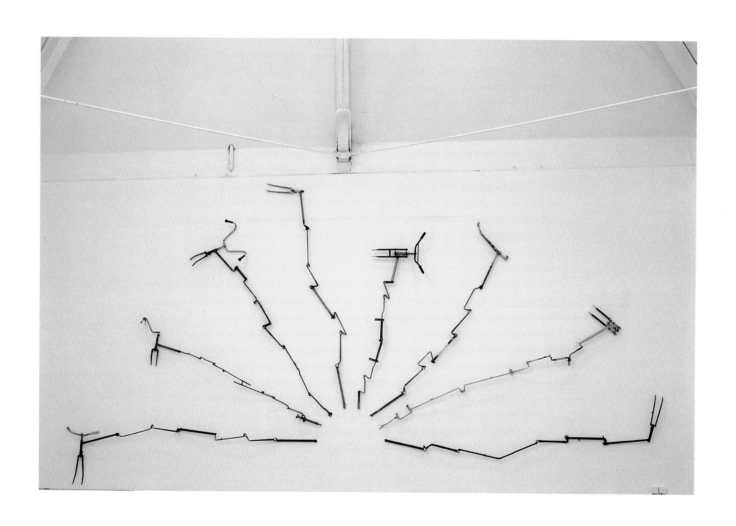

Red Squirrel   1981
electric clothes drying cabinet, acrylic paint
85×50×50 cm.
art & project, Amsterdam
(BW 35)

Twin Tub with Guitar　1980
twin tub washing machine
89×760×660 cm.
Trustees of the Tate Gallery London
(BW 27)

Bean Can with Pen Knife   1981
tin can
10.5×7.5×7.5 cm.
Nicola de Maria
(BW 30)

Electric Fire With Yellow Fish   1981
electric fire, enamel and acrylic paint
25×40×25 cm.
Private Collection
(BW 36A)

Tricycle and Tank 1981
tricycle and enamel paint
40×60×40 cm.
Private Collection
(BW 39)

Camera And Lizard   1981
box camera
16×27×13 cm.
Private Collection
(BW 46)

Crow and Carrion   1981
umbrellas
75 × 120 × 120 cm.
Arts Council of Great Britain
(BW 47)

Car Door, Armchair and Incident   1981
car door, armchair and enamel paint
120×300×300 cm.
Private Collection
(BW 48)

Car Door, Ironing Board, Twin Tub with North American Indian Headdress
car door, ironing board, twin tub washing machine
190 cm. high
Trustees of the Tate Gallery, London
(BW 50)

Pram with Fish   1982
perambulator, enamel paint
90×50×120 cm.
Private Collection, Paris
(BW 56)

Bucket, Mop and Lobster   1982
bucket and mop, enamel paint
120×45×60 cm.
Musée de Toulon
(BW 58)

Twin Tub with Satellite 1982
washing machine, enamel paint
280×200×250 cm.
Musée d'Art et d'Histoire de Chambery
(BW 66)

The Plough and the Rose 1983
car bonnets, enamel and acrylic paint
115×600×500 cm.
Fonds Regional d'Art Contemporain, Rhône-Alpes, Lyon
(BW 79)

Blue Bird, Black Bomb 1983
ironing board, acrylic paint
175×40×210 cm.
Moderna Museet Stockholm, on extended loan from the Beijer Collection
(BW 93)
at *A Pierre et Marie*, Rue d'Ulm, Paris

Red Telephone   1983
car bonnet, enamel paint
120×120×40 cm.
Private Collection
(BW 94)

Quattro Freccie   1983
car bonnet, car door, enamel paint
180×500×80 cm.
Fonds Regional d'Art Contemporain de Bourgogne, Dijon
(BW 96)

Boeing   1983
car door, clothes and suitcase, enamel paint
180×320×180 cm.
Lisson Gallery, London
(BW 97)

Kimono   1983
car bonnets
250×250×250 cm.
art & project, Amsterdam
(BW 102)

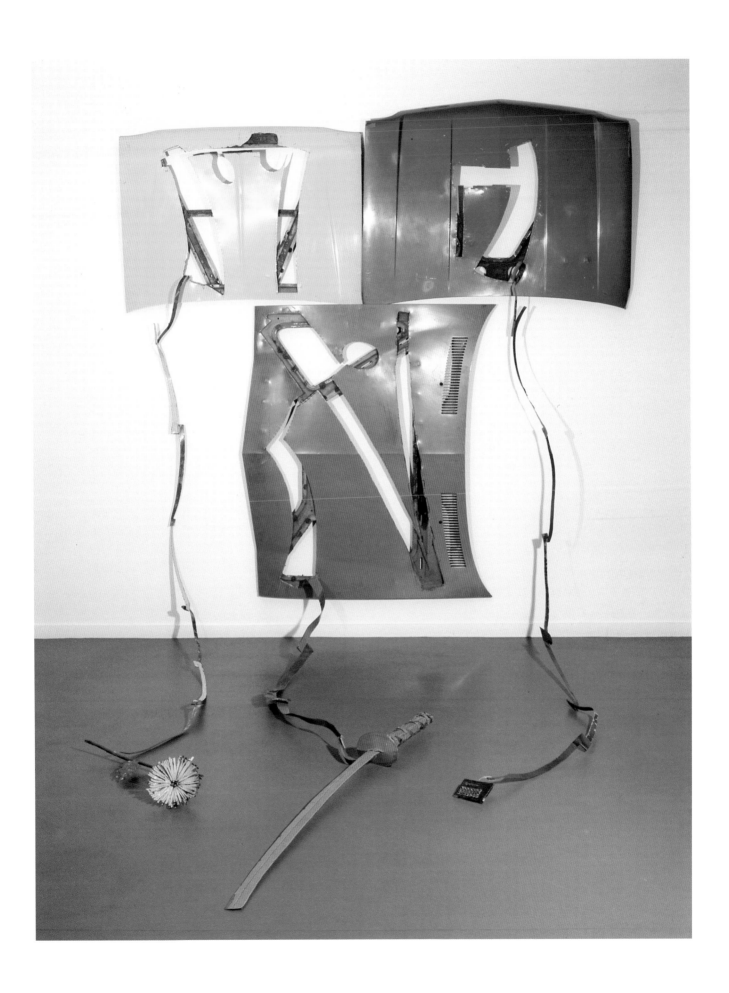

Sea Lion 1983
car bonnets, enamel paint
220×130×100 cm.
Private Collection, Belgium
(BW 104)

Songs of Praise 1983
washing machines, spin dryer, acrylic and enamel paint
140×230×230 cm.
Paul Maenz, Cologne
(BW 105)

The Three Locks 1983
car panels, vacuum cleaners and wooden wardrobe
300×168×86 cm.
Lisson Gallery, London
(BW 113)

Life on Earth 1983
chairs, washing machine, paper, enamel paint
size according to installation
National Gallery of Canada, Ottawa
(BW 114)

Tattoo   1983
car door, car panel, coats
112×160×220 cm.
Private Collection, New York
(BW 119)

Cello Chicken   1983
two car bonnets
150×300×300 cm.
Lisson Gallery, London
(BW 123)

Lower East Side Lintel   1983
steel locker, tyres, coat, car bonnets, enamel paint
250×175×120 cm.
Collection Mr. and Mrs. Arthur Goldberg, New York
(BW 125)

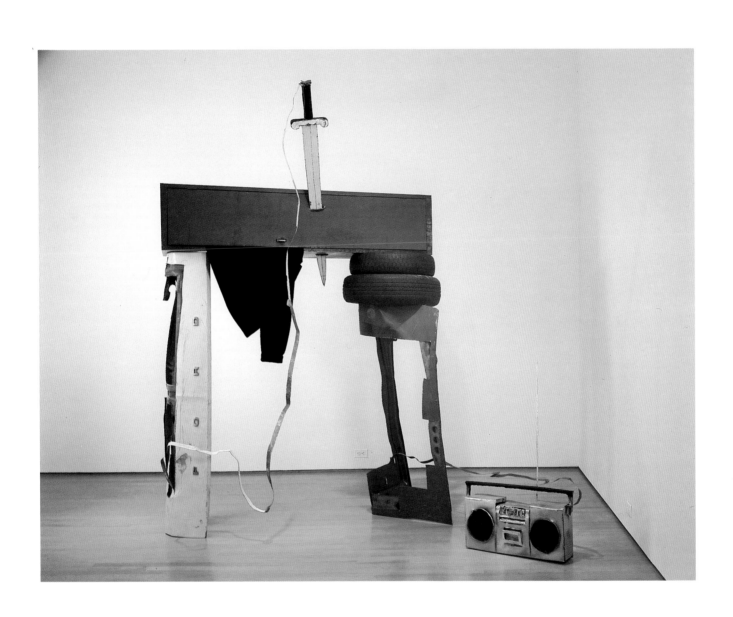

Table   1983
car bonnet, acrylic and spray paint
110×140×120 cm.
Paul Maenz, Cologne
(BW 127)

Table with Locust and Reliquary   1983
car bonnet, enamel and acrylic paint
600×860×984 cm.
Locus Solus, Genoa
(BW 130)

Hawaiian Punch   1983
car bonnet, acrylic and spray paint
100×120×40 cm.
Private Collection
(BW 127A)

Albero e Uccello   1983
olive oil cans
250×150×130 cm.
Rijksmuseum Kröller-Müller, Otterlo
(BW 128)
photographed in Artimino, Tuscany

Il Prete   1983
charity collection box and bed-warmer frame
75×55×200 cm.
Private Collection, Paris
(BW 129)

La Lacrima   1983
industrial gas light reflector, enamel and acrylic paint
70×50×50 cm.
Private Collection
(BW 132)

Water Bird   1983
frying pan
25×40×11 cm.
Private Collection
(BW 134B)

The Glass Jar   1983
tea pot, glass jar, acrylic paint
28×31×20 cm.
Private Collection
(BW 135)

Soupe du Jour   1983
saucepan, ladle, enamel paint
28×39×22 cm.
Private Collection
(BW 136)

◀ *Parrot Fashion*   1983
car bonnet, outboard motor, enamel and acrylic paint
210×210×120 cm.
Musée d'Art Contemporain, Montreal
(BW 139)

Cage　1984
car bonnet, fire extinguisher, enamel paint
90×200×150 cm.
Lisson Gallery, London
(BW 150)

Elephant 1984
car doors and panels, vacuum cleaner, ironing board, wall maps, enamel paint
360×700×360 cm.
Janet Green Collection, London
(BW 154)

One, Nine, Eight, Four 1984
collating machine, wooden cabinet
250×122×120 cm.
Lisson Gallery, London
(BW 156)

Golden Calf 1984
guitar case and anatomical model of cow, metal box, enamel paint
96×89×110 cm.
Lisson Gallery, London
(BW 157)

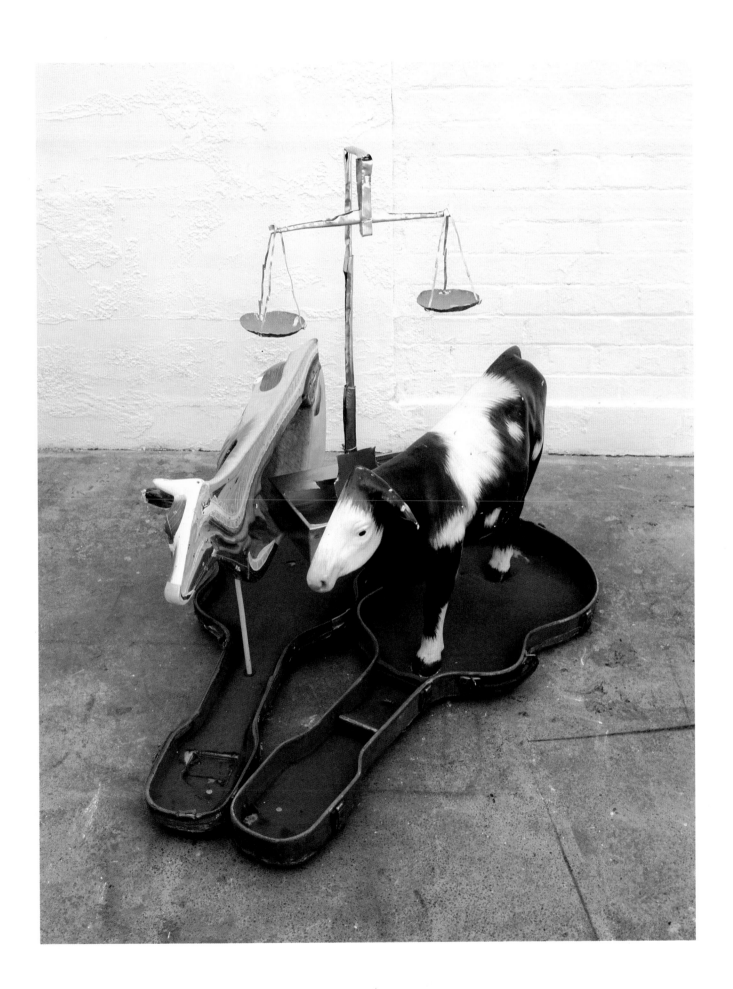

Ship of Fools, Figure of Gold   1984
car bonnet with chrome stand, enamel paint
160×90×120 cm.
Sammlung Wolf, Essen
(BW 158)

Sunset 1984
car bonnet, table, enamel paint
175×130×65 cm.
Lisson Gallery, London
(BW 160)

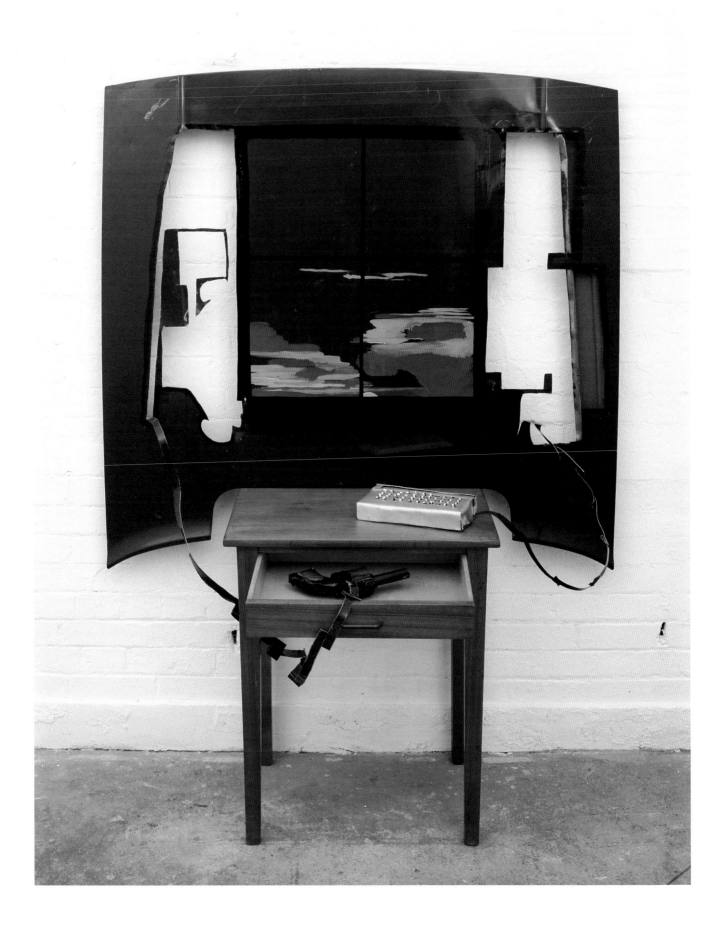

Ship of Fools, Colour of Night   1984
umbrellas
135×200×250 cm.
Sammlung Thomas, Munich
(BW 161)

Blue Monkey 1984
couch, motor scooter, car bonnet, metal box, acrylic paint
405×100×300 cm.
Paul Maenz, Cologne
(BW 162)

Black Magic, White Tricks   1984
car bonnets, enamel paint
150×310×60 cm.
Private Collection, San Francisco
(BW 163)

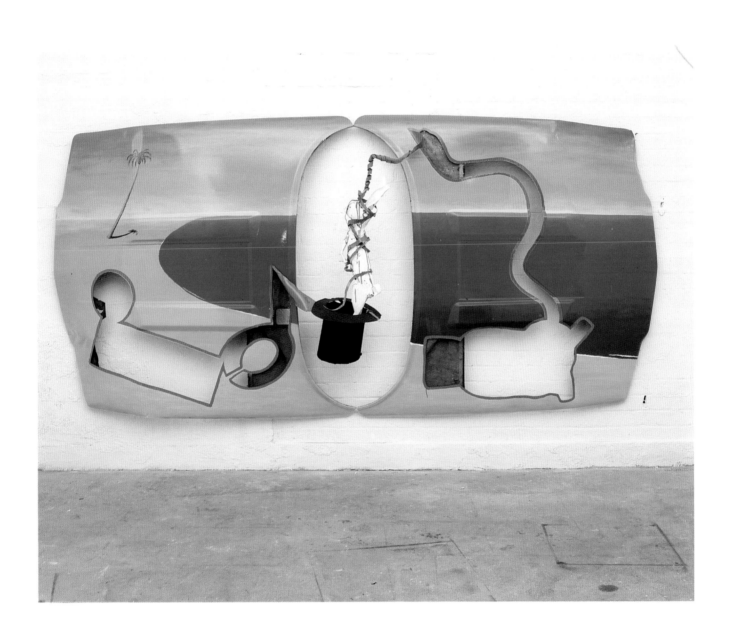

L'Usine, l'Usine   1984
Renault 25 estate car bodies, car bonnets, acrylic paint
490×650×150 cm.
Janet Green Collection, London
(BW 168)

Ship of Fools, Soil for the Tiller   1984
car doors, car bonnet and fabric, enamel paint
150×220×550 cm.
Ray Hughes Gallery, Sydney
(BW 171)

Red Monkey   1985
filing cabinet with spray enamel and bowling balls
224×174×838 cm.
Barbara Gladstone Gallery, New York and Lisson Gallery, London
(BW 172)

Leaf 1985
aeroplane wing, filing cabinet, car panels, acrylic and enamel paint
160×380×555 cm.
Barbara Gladstone Gallery, New York and Lisson Gallery, London
(BW 174)

Time and Place for Nothing   1985
wooden dressers, filing cabinet drawers
328×126×132 cm.
Barbara Gladstone Gallery, New York and Lisson Gallery, London
(BW 175)

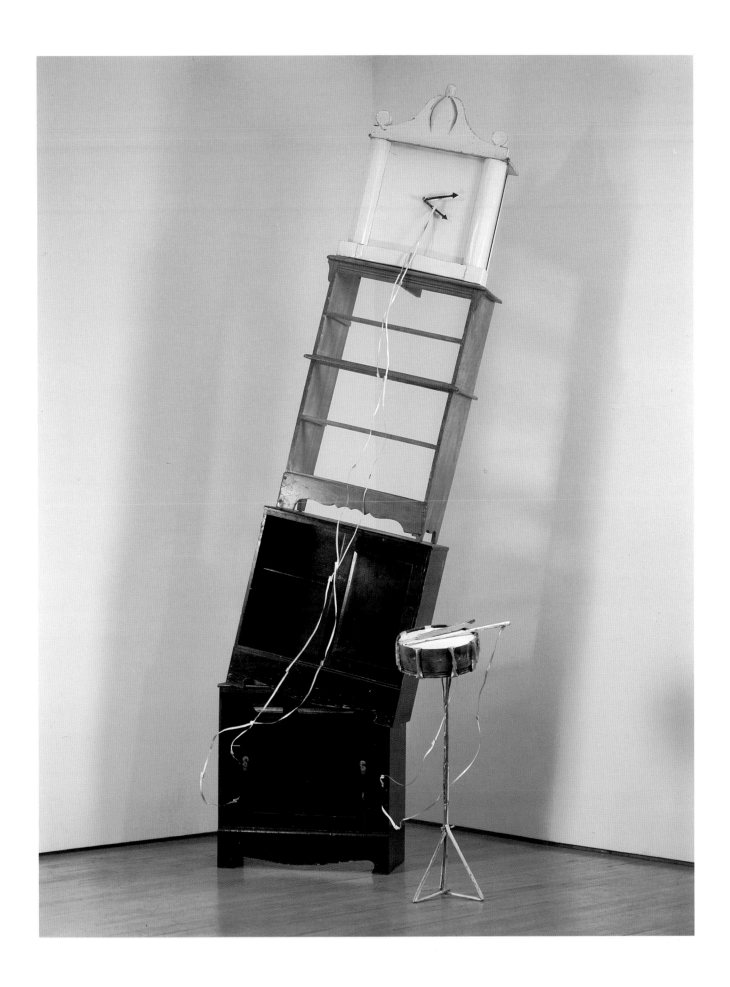

Ship of Fools, Captain's Table   1985
car bonnet, table, chair, enamel and acrylic paint
150×220×220 cm.
Private Collection, New York
(BW 177)

Green Snake   1985
cymbal stand, enamel paint
138×54×49 cm.
Private Collection
(BW 193)

Still Waters   1985
car bonnets, bedbox springs, enamel and acrylic paint
120×300×500 cm.
La Jolla Museum of Contemporary Art, La Jolla, California
(BW 196)

Trivial Pursuits   1985
car door, enamel and acrylic paint
90×130×65 cm.
Michael Krichman and Leslie Simon Collection
(BW 197)

Fools' Coats 1985
coats, breadbox, metal box, cocktail shaker, metal board, enamel and acrylic paint
203×151×79 cm.
Gerald W. Bush Collection, Concord, Massachusetts
(BW 199)

Promised Land   1985
steel office cabinets, car bonnets, men's jackets, enamel paint
465×397×351 cm.
Museum of Art, Carnegie Institute, Pittsburgh
(BW 205)

Switch   1986
toy horse, metal trunk, car bonnet, enamel and acrylic paint
143×187×300 cm.
Mr. and Mrs. Werner Dannheisser Collection, New York
(BW 208)

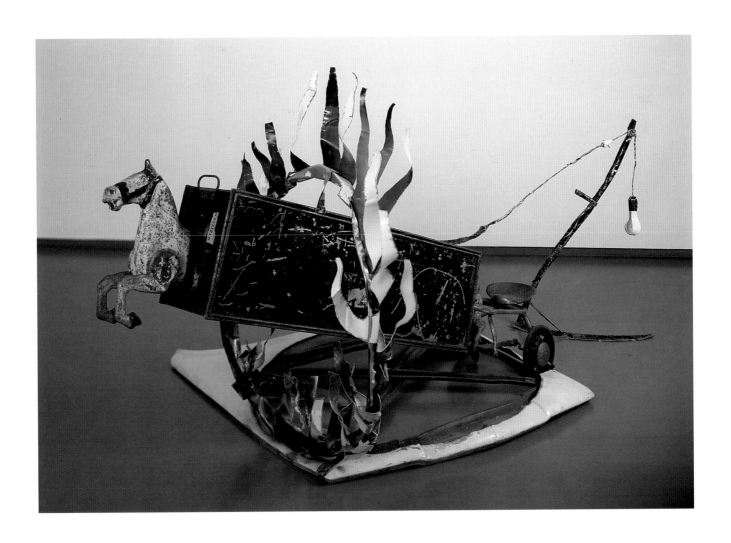

By the Light of Day 1986
metal shelving unit, enamel and acrylic paint
273×115×69 cm.
Paul Maenz, Cologne
(BW 209)

The Golden Rule   1986
filing cabinet, car bonnet, wooden boat, shovel, enamel paint
290×180×185 cm.
Galerie Nordenhake, Stockholm
(BW 210)

Winter Jacket   1986
metal trunk, wall map
131×215×184 cm.
Anne-Marie Walker Collection, Tiburin, California
(BW 215)

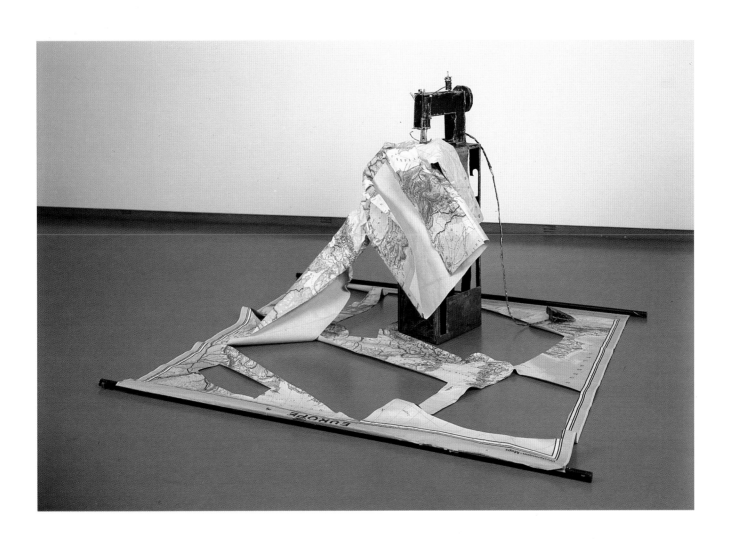

Achtung! 1986
car bonnets, enamel paint
135×410×180 cm.
Sammlung Ackermanns, Xanten
(BW 217)

Ship of Fools, Belly of the Beast   1986
aluminium bath tub, enamel paint
64×190×95 cm.
Paul Maenz, Cologne
(BW 218)

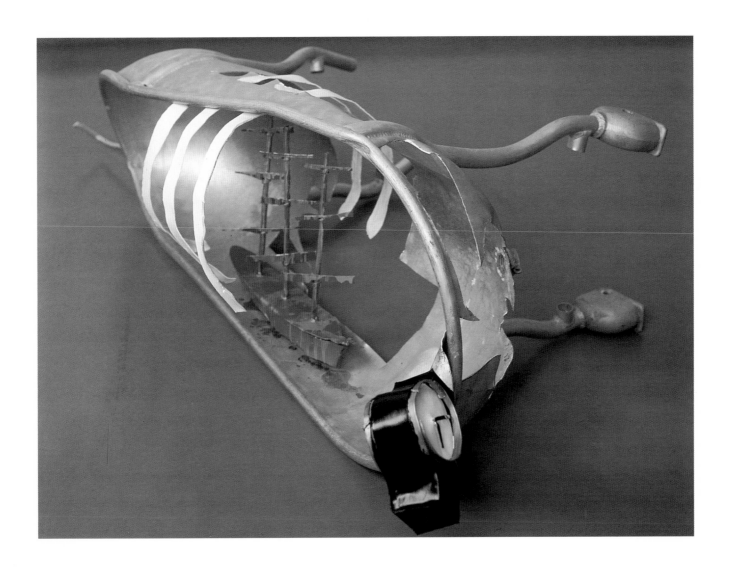

Self-Portrait in the Nuclear Age   1986
shelving unit, wooden box, globe, wall map, coat, acrylic paint
202×250×184 cm.
Lisson Gallery, London
(BW 227)